A
Shepherd's
Yarns

Devotional Talks

by JENNY SPARKS

MOORLEY'S Print & Publishing

Illustrations by
Rebecca Johnson
(Bluecoat School, Nottingham)

MOORLEY'S Print & Publishing

23 Park Rd., Ilkeston, Derbys DE7 5DA
✄   Tel/Fax: (0115) 932 0643   ✄

ISBN 0 86071 478 0

CONTENTS

MOORLEY'S

are growing Publishers, adding several new titles to our list each year. We also undertake private publications and commissioned works.

Our range of publications includes: **Books of Verse**
Devotional Poetry
Recitations
Drama
Bible Plays
Sketches
Nativity Plays
Passiontide Plays
Easter Plays
Demonstrations
Resource Books
Assembly Material
Songs & Musicals
Children's Addresses
Prayers & Graces
Daily Readings
Books for Speakers
Activity Books
Quizzes
Puzzles
Painting Books
Daily Readings
Church Stationery
Notice Books
Cradle Rolls
Hymn Board Numbers

Please send a S.A.E. (approx 9" x 6") for the current catalogue or consult your local Christian Bookshop who should stock or be able to order our titles.

MATILDA

Why are you cast down O my soul...? Hope in God; for I shall again praise Him, my help and my God Psalm 43.5.

Is lying on your back in the sun your idea of bliss? If you were a sheep it definitely would NOT be, in fact it would be sheer hell, as you will see. But first I must introduce Matilda, who is an expert on the subject. She used to belong to a friend of mine who was  offered a partnership on a Devon farm. Penelope was very excited about the move, but there was one cloud on her horizon. If you are imagining one of those white, fluffy, billowing cumulus that scud across the sky, forget it! No. Penelope's cloud was in the shape of Matilda, her favourite ewe. Matilda is white certainly, but light and buoyant she is not! Weighty and wedge-shaped, she looks as though all her suspension has collapsed. As someone once remarked in hushed tones: "She's lost her figure". Truly, I don't think she ever had one because in all the years I have known her - she is now 12 - she has always looked several months pregnant. When she actually IS in-lamb, her back view is nothing short of amazing.

But it was not Matilda's shape that worried Penelope (although perhaps it ought to have done), it was what Matilda got up to - or rather down to - that concerned her. If you knew Matilda you could not imagine her getting up to anything much; she is dignified and stately, with a particularly refined bleat and keeps her children firmly in check, not wanting them to mix with the riff-raff. So what **does** Matilda do? Well, you must picture her taking her ease, lying on her front, when she gets an itch. She writhes, turns on her side, leans round just a bit too far, and.... ooops, over she goes. Her sagging figure flops out and she becomes so wide that she is stranded upside-down, unable to rise. "Cast down" in a shepherd's terms. All she can do is wait for rescue and hope we will come quickly.

When I agreed to look after Matilda, I had no idea how good she was at this trick. Often she is over three times a day in the itchy season, and so a continual watch must be placed on her. She also has the gift of choosing bad moments - like the morning she somehow managed to flop over in the path of an escaping bullock. As it took us an hour to catch up with him, Matilda had to be left where she was.

Another time she missed out on all the fun, when the entire flock escaped and the only sheep we had left was an upside-down Matilda. Had she gone to Devon, where the 200 acres consist of long, lush grass, she would never have been spotted in time and would have died long ago, because, of course, a cast sheep is a doomed sheep. Lying on its back, the rumen (the first huge stomach) presses on its lungs and fluid builds up in which it slowly drowns. The gases cannot escape from the rumen and these will also choke the sheep. Survival time varies greatly - Matilda is so used to it happening to her that she does not panic. She stays calm, trusting in our rescue and this has kept her alive, whereas others have died in an hour or so, their frantic struggles adding to their problems. There is nothing more distressing or depressing for a shepherd than a dead, cast sheep. It is such an unnecessary death, worse still if it was heavily in-lamb. If ever you see a sheep in this position, run and help her at once!

In the Psalms, David continually refers back to his shepherding days, and in Nos. 42 and 43, he is picturing Matilda's plight. He wants us to see that our Shepherd is yearning to rescue us when our souls are "cast down", His hand outstretched to restore us and set us onto our feet again to walk with Him. We have only to cry out to Him and take His hand - He is waiting for our S.O.S. Do we feel in the depths of despair, abandoned, beyond help, just like Matilda? Remember she does not give up hope; she even bleats for us in her own distinctive voice, which I can recognise a quarter of a mile away. If she is prepared to trust in me like this, how much more should we trust in our Lord and His deliverance. He WILL rescue us - "hope still in God" - think of Paul, he knew enough of tribulation and despair, but he had proved that "God comforts the downcast", 2 Corinthians verse 6. So let us reverse the situations we find ourselves in and "cast all our cares on Him, because He cares for us", 1 Peter 5 verse 7.

THE CALLING

"My sheep hear my voice and I know them and they follow me"

John Chapter 10 verse 27.

As Jesus spoke those words, there was probably a shepherd in sight calling to his sheep and all the crowd would have instantly related to this parable. Modern day flocks here in East Anglia are worked with dogs and the shepherds seldom, if ever, call to their sheep. I've always talked to mine and led them everywhere by voice, even when we had a flock of 150 strong and there came a day when I was very glad I had done so.

I happened to be feeding the cattle and milking the house cow, when I heard a commotion. Dramas usually occur when my hands are full, especially literally so, when I am hand-milking. "I'll have to go", I said to the cows, "I think there's something wrong". Running to the house with the pail of milk, I saw our neighbouring farmer roaring past in his pick-up, he was making for the stubble field opposite, where I was strip grazing my sheep. He began tooting his horn and shouting, which meant he was trying to round up his sheep. To my horror I realised they must have escaped, yet again, and had reached our land this time.

Filling a bucket with some carrots I ran the half mile across the lane to the stubble field which was not an easy task as it was uphill, over a ploughed area, and to cap it all, it was pouring with rain. As I neared the spot where my sheep should have been I could see that their electric netting was down and they had gone. Further ahead I could see that the farmer and three of his men were rounding up his flock in a corner of the field, preparatory to driving them off. I suppose he had about seventy ewes at that time and somewhere in the midst of them were mine as well. "Stop! Wait!" I called several times as I puffed up the field. At some point on the way I tripped up, shooting all the carrots out of the pail. All the while I was running, my concern for my ewes was growing. I was sure that my neighbour was planning to drive my sheep with his the mile back to his farm. I could not let this happen since they were only two weeks off lambing and would not have coped with the speed, length and harshness of such a journey. I just had to separate them out and I was determined to do so. As I approached the terrified huddle of animals I knew there was no doubt in my mind about the action I had to take (I suppose I was going to exercise the sort of "*faith which moves mountains*" Mark II 23, ie: major problems).

"I want my sheep out of there," I shouted as I reached them all.

"You'll never get yours out of that bunch," laughed the men, "go away and leave this to us."

"I certainly **will** get them out," I insisted, "stand back all of you, keep out of the way and watch."

I now realised that to call my sheep, I must use the name they were familiar with. It was a bit unfortunate that at that time the flock were known as 'The Woollies', (a child who had been visiting had thus christened them and the name had stuck as names sometimes do!)

Feeling a bit sheepish, but nevertheless determined to rescue my sheep, I put a few stones in my now empty bucket and rattled it.

"Woollies," I called, "come on Woollies, this way."

For a few moments there was no response, although I could see faces I knew in the midst of the huge flock. Then, one by one, led by an old faithful ewe, they began to elbow their way out of the crowd and come to me. A few of my neighbour's sheep came too as we began to set off down the hill. Then I realised that I had not got Claude, my ram, because he had been somewhat dazed and distracted by the appearance of seventy new wives!

I couldn't turn back otherwise my ewes would have returned as well, so I asked the men to shout at him. Their unfamiliar yells spurred him into action and he hurtled out to join me, vividly illustrating verse 45 of John 10 '*they will flee from a stranger*'. He was literally scared out of his wits and so out of the escaped bunch. Once he was at my side we could all finally set off back home to calm down and recover.

My sheep had truly heard my voice and followed me, when it really mattered. But how much more important it is for us to know our Shepherd's voice so that we can follow His leading. We cannot know what events or crises will come our way, but if we will follow His Path we have nothing to fear. We need to ask for His leading at the start of each day and set **"Our Lord always ahead of us"** just as David says in Psalm 16, verse 8. If only we could be like my sheep who are always ready to follow me and daily do so. They are in the habit of expecting my calling. And Our Lord wants us to be in the same state of readiness, so like David **"we shall put him at our right hand** and **whatever happens we shall not be moved"**.

FOR HIS NAME'S SAKE

We shepherds are a funny lot. Our lifestyle tends to make us fiercely independent and self-reliant, and the loneliness can even make us rather reclusive. On the other hand, where our sheep are concerned, we are surprisingly affected by the opinion of others. There is nothing which satisfies us more than to see our flocks, especially ewes and lambs together, looking content and well-cared for, happily grazing in a well-kept pasture. If you have ever wondered about the uses we make of our crooks, put "propping up a tired but proud shepherd" at the top of the list.

However, when we are doing this, we are also looking for any signs of trouble. Why? Well, sheep and their problems would fill an Encyclopaedia and are just too much for general knowledge. But one Autumn I rather wished I had aired at least the basics with a friend of mine. He kept a few young ewes and asked if he could borrow a ram for them. As it happened, I had a very tame six month old ram lamb and was hoping to find a good home for him. Even at such a tender age, young Henry was a fine husband for 6 nubile wives and they welcomed him with open 'arms'.

He was to stay with them for two or three months, and having seen him settle in, I happily left him in his new home.

It was a busy time for me on the farm, and I have to admit that Henry was far from my mind for the next few weeks. But an urgent telephone call one lunch time was to bring him right to the fore again. It was my friend.

"I'm a bit worried about the ram, I've tried to help him, but he's very poorly and I wish you would come over."

"What's the matter?" I asked anxiously. "Well..... he's had lots of trouble from flies and lost some of his fleece and now he's just lying about doing nothing."

"Do you mean he is Fly Struck?"

"Yeeess... but I've treated the maggots, its not just that.. ."

"We'll come at once," I interrupted him, and going outside called out to Michael to get the van out. On our arrival at my friend's field, we could see Henry lying under a tree, neck outstretched, looking very ill and dejected. On examining him I became both shocked and VERY ANGRY. What I had taken to be attached wool, just came away in my hands, revealing rotting flesh and raw wounds, and these also continued down his back legs. Further along his body where he still had some fleece, there were hundreds, perhaps thousands, of maggots happily buried and eating him alive. I had never seen such a bad strike.

"I've poured neat Jeyes Fluid on his back and killed the maggots there," said my friend, trying to reassure me. So **now** I understood why the ram's flesh was a strange leathery brown in places. Just imagine what agony he must have undergone! Neat burning Jeyes on huge open wounds!! Fighting back a violent outburst, I turned to Michael and without replying we lifted Henry up and put him straight into the van. He was close to death and was certainly no use to his young wives now.

Once back on the farm, I made up a solution of dip which I poured over the patches of maggots - these had to be killed before we could help the ram in any other way. Although very weak he managed to stand while the dip did its work, and at last he was rid of that ghastly writhing nightmare. I decided to put him on some shaded grass opposite the house by the lane, so that I could keep an eye on him and go to him as often as possible.

Like all my sheep he was very fond of bread, so over the next few days we got through several loaves, and whenever I took him a treat it was also an opportunity to give him some love. I sat and talked with him and stroked his face, while he lay weak and shocked. Slowly he began to respond and take an interest in his surroundings and finally after 3 or 4 days he started to graze. His dreadful wounds took a long while to heal and eventually he lost over half his fleece, revealing the full extent of the horrors he had undergone.

One day, while I was with him, a farmer neighbour who also keeps sheep, pulled up. He had spotted the ram and could not resist asking about him. However had I let him get into such a state? He had thought I was a better shepherd than that! I hastily gave him an account of what had happened, seeing that my 'good name' was at stake, because every shepherd knows that sheep and their condition mirror the one who cares for them. This is because unlike any other livestock they are so vulnerable and dependent. Until that moment I don't think I had actually considered the care of my sheep in that light; I had just done my best for them because I love them, but I know I would have been very ashamed of myself if the ram had suffered so badly under my management. The whole episode gave me an insight into My Shepherd's position.

All **His** provision, which we can find encapsulated in Psalm 23, is so great that "we shall never want"; so like loved-for sheep we should be glowing with spiritual health, and that in turn, means we should be reflecting His care and His character for **His** sake, not ours. He wants to be proud of His sheep too, and He wants others outside His flock to be attracted and drawn to Him by seeing us.

Do I reflect His love, patience, trust, loyalty, courage, joy? I know to my shame I am so often a very poor mirror image and the worst of it is that others **do** notice. Like a sheep who is a poor doer, my failures will stick out like a sore thumb. I've always found that the scraggy ewe is the one who comes to the gate first for all to see! And my reaction to her is to feel ashamed. Praise God that Our Shepherd is not like that - He is long-suffering, ready to restore us even when we let Him down. Not only that but He is still prepared to trust us, because He sees the best in us, and knows that under His continuing care we can fulfil our true potential for him.

BELLA

Bella is a magnificent Red Poll cow - "good enough to show", pronounced one farming friend. Yes, but sadly her looks are not matched by her brains. She is in the 'Dumb Blonde' mould and one glance at her eyes tells all. They are tiny and are set very high up in her head, and are perpetually registering total confusion. While the rest of the Herd will listen and follow me, quickly summing up any new situation, Bella becomes bewildered and panicky. Without the others she goes completely to pieces

and although she knows her name, she can't respond. Not only is she dim-witted but she is also not very good at calving.

The birth of her first son made one New Year's Eve a nightmare for us and for her. He was eventually winched out backwards, more dead than alive. He had to be hung up over a hay rack to have his lungs drained of all the fluid he had swallowed and then undergo heart massage before he finally revived. His mother was so muddled up by all this that she rejected him for some hours, and by the time she got round to loving and licking him, he was too weak to stand and suckle. That meant hand feeding for some days until he grew stronger.

Her second calving was uneventful, but she decided to produce her third offspring one perishing October afternoon out on the field where the Herd were staying until winter set in.

It soon became apparent that she was in difficulties and as I knew that she would never be persuaded to come back to the building alone we would have to catch her and help her out there. But how? She was getting frightened and, of course, confused, and so when I tried to halter her she made a dash for it. This despite the fact that bits of baby were by now well out. If you have ever tried to keep pace with over half a ton of pounding bovine on the end of rope you can picture the scene. My feet scarcely touched the ground and in the end I did not keep up, let alone win the race and the halter was wrenched from my grasp as I slipped despairingly in a cowpat. A friend who had come to help me had just eaten a large meal of fish and chips and his attempts to help were making him not only share my frustration but feel sick as well!

After fifteen minutes she paused for breath, long enough for us to get a better grip on both the rope and baby, which we then pulled out, while Bella had a rest and refused to help us. Naturally enough, the youngster had not enjoyed all this and lay exhausted, unable to rise while his mother half-heartedly agreed to lick and dry him.

A cup of tea soon revived me, but I knew the Bella episode was far from over. Baby was too weak to be left out in the wind and rain, even if he ever got up to suck. Somehow I would have to bring him and his mum back to the buildings, but however would I persuade her to leave the Herd? I could only hope she would follow Baby, and as they were a quarter of a mile from the farm, I decided to take a wheelbarrow out in which to transport the calf. Once I was back with them I put the barrow on its side and rolled the infant, who weighed about sixty pounds into it, and somehow hauled the whole lot upright. So far so good; now to get Bella and the "pram" out through the gate without all the Herd following. This too worked like clockwork. But after that the rot set in; I found that Bella would only follow if I wheeled Baby backwards, so she could see him clearly. It was slow and painful work as the infant would keep lurching about and the pram wobbled alarmingly. To reach our goal we had to go along a track which leads through a piece of woodland and here we ran into more trouble. Nothing would persuade Mother to join us; "Didn't I know there were ghosts and monsters waiting to get her in there?" After several false starts I became exasperated and dumped Baby on the track and set off for some 'bait'. Returning with a sack of carrots I unceremoniously tipped these in the barrow around and even on top of the youngster. Holding one out to Bella, who grabbed it eagerly, I then inched the pram backwards as she took one after another and forgot her fears.

At last we were at the buildings and into the Cattle Yard, where I slammed the gate to and wheeled the now very sorry looking infant into a Loose Box and tipped him out onto some straw. The journey had taken some thirty minutes and this meant Baby was now about two hours old and it was high time he had his first drink of life-saving Colostrum. Here I met another snag, Bella absolutely refused to let me milk any of hers out: I had no choice but to go to the house for some of the frozen stuff I always keep for emergencies, and thaw it out as soon as possible.

Another twenty minutes later I was back in the Loose Box with the vital bottle trying to stuff the teat into Baby's unwilling mouth. It was soon obvious he was never going to suck. I needed a stomach tube, but I only possessed a lamb-sized one. I rushed off to phone a neighbour, but no, he didn't have one either. I'd got to get milk down the calf somehow and then I remembered some soft rubber tubing I had found in Michael's shed.

Guessing a suitable length, I rinsed it out, stuck a very large syringe on the end, and set off once again for the farm. Baby objected violently to being force fed but eventually most of the first litre went down. I had to repeat this treatment for two more feeds and then to my relief he sucked the first feed the next morning and by the afternoon he was up and sucking from his Mum. Having overcome so many hurdles, he just had to be called Pascoe, after our famous Olympic hurdler, and despite such a poor start, he too, triumphed and grew into a fine animal.

Life for many of us can also seem like one obstacle course after another and problems always seem to come in bunches. In Jesus' short years of ministry, He faced one difficulty after another and He took great pains to frequently warn His disciples that their lives would be full of troubles if they followed Him. He never promised that the Christian life would be easy or comfortable and Paul certainly knew the cost of serving His Lord; one glance at the list of trials he suffered and which we can find in 2 Corinthians 11: 23-27 would make us see our own problems in a different light. Peter tells us in 1 Peter 2: 20-21, that we are **called** to suffer for Christ's sake, and James tells us in James 1.2. *"Count it all joy"* when we suffer trials. That is a very tall order for most of us, and I know my instinctive reaction is to grumble, and feel angry, even bitter. I certainly had all these responses during three dreadful years of problems which ended in Michael's death. But the Lord showed me that He wanted me to endure hardness so that He would make me a braver and stronger soldier who would not fall at the first hurdle. He wants all of us, who have committed ourselves to His service, to be ready to stand for Him through thick and thin, through the bad as well as the good times, and to be ready to strengthen and encourage others.

And he does not expect us to stand alone in our trials; He has made so many promises to be with us, giving us comfort and power to cope. "His everlasting arms are underneath us" carrying us through everything we shall face - not some old wheelbarrow but God's own Hands are bearing us up! By giving us trials God is giving us a 'Vote of

Confidence', trusting us to keep our faith in Him through anything and witness to His Loving Care. For we know that in God's eternal plans for us "**all** things work together for our good", even if we cannot understand things at this moment in time.

THE FATAL FLAW

Broad is the road that leads to destruction   Matthew 7.13.

All classes of sheep are walking disaster areas, but none more so than the lambs which have the unhappy knack of being accident prone on top of their predilection for any disease going. They can actually be in trouble from the moment of conception, because their mothers walk such a narrow tightrope during multiple pregnancies.

This results in us poor shepherds having some nasty surprises at their delivery. Mummification, putrefaction and deformities are all to be found. But it is once they are born alive that the real troubles start. Did you know that 4 million lambs die every spring in the U.K., usually within one week of birth? This does include death at lambing too - and you can well imagine that twins, triplets or quads can easily become tangled up in their struggle to arrive first, so that malpresentations result in many still-births.

Once they have taken their first look at this world, some lambs wish they had stayed where they were in the womb and they quickly decide it is all far too much effort to live. Large lowland lambs are especially dozy and reluctant to have to get up and find Mother's teat. It's much easier to just lie there and die! **GREAT PATIENCE AND CONTORTIONS**

are the basic requirements for shepherds at these times. Just picture trying to hold a lamb on to a tiny teat while it refuses to suck, underneath a ewe who won't stand still, while you are kneeling in what I don't want to describe! I have often reached the stage of shaking the ewe at this point!

Then I have to resort to forced feeding via a stomach tube which is essential practice if you are going to thwart the lamb's suicide plans. With those infants who are deceptively vigorous at birth the shepherd needs extra vigilance. For their first 24 hours they are the targets of a host of bugs, and one in particular which bumps up that 4 million total is the aptly named 'watery mouth'. This is an E.Coli stomach bug which not even mother's colostrum anti-bodies will kill off. Within a few hours afflicted lambs blow up like little balloons and fade very quickly. Every infant has an anti-biotic pill at birth on my farm and then frequent checks to see if its chin is dry. A dribbly mouth is a dire sign.

Up to a week old the favourite way of dying is by hypothermia; the tinier the lamb the more it is at risk, especially in cold, wet spells. Shelter is a must and some kind of warming device needs to be at the ready. My Rayburn ovens have often been pressed into service, but care is needed to avoid roasting the little mite!

There are also many bizarre causes of death, like being squashed by Mother for example. This is likely if she is finding it difficult to get up and down after a bad birth. One Spring seemed to be the 'season of the squashed lamb' here, when I lost two fine infants, flattened like pancakes by their ageing Mums. I nearly lost a third, but arrived on the scene just in time to find a little back leg sticking out from the ewe who had flopped down on Baby before he could scramble out of the way. This lamb was a very strange shape for a couple of hours - very wasp-waisted and fighting for breath; but it slowly filled out to its normal size and amazingly survived.

Another favourite suicide trick is to get into Mother's water bucket, curl up and quietly drown. Other lambs who are the introverted type, force themselves into impossibly narrow gaps, get jammed and can't find reverse gear. Chilling or starvation can overtake them.

Others relish trying to strangle themselves in the fencing or the ewes' hay nets or racks. I have even had a lamb run over by a portable hay feeder, 10' by 3', which the ewes can manage to push all round the field. And a shepherd friend crossed his heart and told me he had found a dead lamb which had apparently been trying to eat a mole trap.

Older lambs can do equally daft things and are also prey to the staggers and pulpy kidney (if not vaccinated). This fatal disease is again triggered by stress; the E. Welchi bug is in the soil and therefore in their intestines. A change of diet or an event like shearing when ewes and lambs are handled and panicked or a violent storm can be the cause of an outbreak.

Worm infestation which builds up in lambs of three months or more can also kill if not treated, and on fenced lowland grazing it is almost impossible to avoid this problem. Mountain sheep, who are always on the move, again escape such problems. And it is certainly possible to kill lambs with kindness - give them a lush, high protein, clover rich sward and you can expect bloat. That sounds like a nasty bout of indigestion, but it is much worse than that because like all ruminants sheep have four stomachs. Alka Seltzer won't help them because the problem occurs in stomach No. 1, the Rumen, a huge fermenting organ, where the hastily grazed food is composted. If the food is very rich and gassy, the sheep's opening to the Rumen becomes blocked. It then cannot burp out the gas and it will literally blow up and die.

With all these possibilities to face, it is no wonder that it is difficult to amaze shepherds - we've seen it all and more. And since the commonest sign of trouble is sudden death, we have to be prepared to take anything in our stride. We try to plan for every eventuality but we never manage it. The sheep are much cleverer than us and far more determined to kill themselves than we seem to be at saving them.

In our Heavenly Father's eyes, we humans must look just the same. Self-destruction is part of our make-up too, as we run pell mell into every danger area. No human warnings can stop us; from childhood we have to prove ourselves and test everything and everyone around us. We always know best - even in our teens, we are sure we can handle the fast car, the soft drugs, the strong drink, violence and pornography. Even as a nation, we are sure all is in our control, whether it is racism, scientific discoveries, especially nuclear and genetic, or foreign aggression. In our own lives we are unaware that the things we try out can so easily take control of us and even be the death of us. The first time we drive say at 100mph on a motorway we are a bit scared that we may be caught, but then each time after it becomes easier and easier to do and the thrill or addiction or whatever takes us over. The world can soon crowd out human warnings and phrases like 'a Government Health Warning' become so familiar we start to joke about them, sure that 'it will never happen to us'.

So it is hardly surprising that God's warnings are even less heeded; they seem out of touch with the reality around us. Well, it was certainly so in Noah's time; he was laughed to scorn when he told those around him of God's anger and promised judgement of a Global Flood. But 120 years passed by, during which Noah obeyed God and built the Ark, whilst there was no sign of rain and wind. So to everyone around him, his prophecy seemed ridiculous, especially as the climate was quite different at that time, and rain was unknown; instead mists, dews, and springs watered the earth. No wonder people thought Noah was quite crackers and took no notice of his words. Despite this humiliation and mocking Noah's faith was strong throughout those years - 120 **days** would have been too much for me, I know. But God did carry out His words and it is certain that He will bring about His Judgement Day at our Lord Jesus' Second Coming. If you are not convinced, I'll just add this point. Jesus fulfilled the most minute details (as well as the mega ones) of Old Testament prophecies - even to the Roman Soldiers casting lots over his robe at the Crucifixion. The Bible is full of exact dates and historically verifiable facts, which have been proved correct. So it would be surprising if **the** major World event, the end of time for man should be inaccurate. There is no date, but plenty of references to its coming and it is up to us to heed or ignore the warnings. Alongside these is God's way of escape. For Noah, his family and the animal life, it was the Ark, for us it is Our Shepherd's Cross. Instead of continuing on our self-destruction path, we can place our lives into Our Lord's safe keeping.

To save my sheep from all their perils, I have to thrust my rescue plans on them, whether that means a vaccination needle or a worming drench, or controlling their diet. But God won't force Himself on us, instead through circumstances and other means, He reaches out to us. *"Behold, I stand at the door (of our hearts) and knock, if anyone hears my voice and will open the door I will come in and eat with him".* Rev.3 v 20.

He waits for our invitation, and our abandonment of self-reliance. Self-sufficiency is woefully inadequate for sheep as well as for us, may "our sufficiency be of God" instead.

Don't Panic! Don't Panic!

I sought the Lord.... He delivered me from all my fears Psalm 34.4

I have come to the conclusion that my sheep may have been reading the MAFF booklets which thud through my letter box with monotonous regularity. They deserve a medal if they have because these manuals are usually 70 odd pages long and full of Euro gobbledygook. My head starts spinning after just one sentence, especially when it goes something like this.... "if you wish to apply for BSPA SCPS HLCA and SAPS, or require CID's under CAPS, please check your RSC or DO to see if we do not need further

information". Then foreign phrases start cropping up - the favourite being "force majeure". If you bring that into an application, it's rather like invoking an Act of God in an insurance claim. It is the loophole we all grasp hold of, when we have problems with our stock subsidy tallies. And if you keep sheep you certainly need one. No sooner have you neatly completed the latest form for the annual ewe premium and confidently filled in, say, 47, in the box for the total claimed, then you go out to find one has dropped dead just as you were sealing the envelope. I'm sure they get together and call for a volunteer to do a bit of "force majeuring" when they know what I'm doing. Illness and calamities seem to have a morbid fascination for them and when this is linked to their total lack of self defence and their perpetual state of anxiety anything can happen.

"Don't worry - it may never happen" is a motto I perhaps ought to have pinned up in the Sheep House. Mind you, it wouldn't really be true because it nearly always **does** happen to sheep. When a farmer friend of mine heard that I planned to start keeping a flock he lent me a suspiciously thick volume on the "Problems and Diseases of Sheep". But even this did not put me off as he was hoping. I tried to tell myself that I would never see such ghastly sounding things as the staggers, enzootic abortion, vibronic abortion, pulpy kidney, foot rot, fly strike, scab, hypoglycaemia, watery mouth, orf and pregnancy toxaemia (I have listed but a fraction of the likely ones to afflict many flocks). But, as you will know, if you have read these yarns, most of these have come my way and some others beside!

Vaccinations for a host of nasties are available, in fact, you could be sticking needles in your sheep almost every week. This state of affairs has come about because in an effort to make the biggest profits in the meat markets we have been very busy "improving" sheep breeds in order to have the most prolific ewes and fleshy lambs. This means that the modern lowland flocks have lost their natural hardiness, because that trait has been bred out. It belongs to wiry, canny little mountain ewes who are prepared to eke out a living on next to nothing in exchange for producing a single, wiry, little lamb. If you want ewes to have multiple births, preferably large triplets, they will lose some of their toughness and independence since they will need much extra feed and shelter for possibly weaker lambs.

They will also be quite likely to have pregnancy disorders, like toxaemia and malpresentations at birth, which unless a shepherd is at hand will mean death to mother and babies. By being pushed almost beyond their physical limits, these ewes' body resources are completely drained, especially in the last three weeks of their gestations, when the lambs grow at an alarming rate.

If at this time high quality food supplies are inadequate, perhaps during a sudden cold snap, the ewe then has to draw on her body fat reserves. Often a breakdown occurs which poisons her system as Ketosis sets in. The first dread signs are a ewe hanging back at feeding time, not eating, lying down too much and finally appearing very nervous as with a nodding head, she circles aimlessly and finally goes blind. Beyond this she will collapse into a coma, from which it is virtually impossible to rouse her, or save her lambs.

Over the years I have unfortunately lost 3 ewes in this way, all of whom were carrying triplets, and I have had other milder cases. Treatment, to be successful, must be started in the very early stages of the disorder. I have often had to make a mad dash for the house, on discovering someone with one or many of the symptoms. I have a medicine 'chest' (actually a cardboard box) there, with a proprietary remedy - this is the standard dehydration and nutrient therapy for malnourished Third World children. Liquid glucose can be used as well and if given in time both work like magic, often within half an hour. However that is not the end of the matter because the ewe will need frequent doses until she lambs and is out of danger.

The two other major disorders of late pregnancy and post-parturition (and being sheep at almost any other time!) are calcium and magnesium deficiencies.

These don't sound very dire, but I can assure you that both can kill in a matter of a few hours. They are triggered by stress, internal or external; if the sheep is more fortunate she will only get calcium loss (which is often termed milk fever, as it is linked with the time when the udder fills up ready for the newborn lambs). It can come on very quickly if a heavily pregnant flock are frightened and made to run. So it is unwise to round them up and treat them harshly.

If they are terrified by some event, like a dog getting into their field and chasing them, they will scatter wildly and in the process their body metabolism goes haywire. Some or many will then go down never to rise again if not given calcium very quickly. If the stress is very great, magnesium deficiency occurs. This condition is aptly described as the staggers, but most shepherds never witness any of this syndrome. Instead they are confronted by a sheep's favourite ploy - sudden death. It is certainly **not** treatable! But perhaps it is just as well, because even at the staggering and twitching stage there is little time to act and if you do, the activity involved in administering the magnesium, indeed your very approach will be the last straw. She is so nervous that your touch will be enough to trigger an instant heart attack. So, this disorder is one where the sheep is literally scared to death and sadly I lost one of my loveliest ewes, Little 16, in this way. She had been one of the kindest, gentlest souls and a wonderful mother to a usually sturdy set of triplets. When she was 8, and only two weeks off lambing, she was grazing in the field which has a disused railway embankment for one of its boundaries. I was about half a mile away on the Home field doing some fence repairs. Above my hammer blows I became aware of a hullabaloo! Looking up, I saw horses and riders, then I distinguished hounds baying and a horn blaring. The local hunt was riding past me and making for the old railway line. "My ewes," I thought. "They will be terrified, I must run to them as quickly as I can, to give them some comfort." Of course I couldn't keep up with the dogs or leading riders and by the time I reached the flock I could see some of the hounds had burst through my electric fence. I shouted to the Master to call them off, which he quickly did and then I turned to talk to my sheep and lead them back to the safety of their wood. Having seen them calm down, I went back to work for half an hour before I decided to just check them again. As I handed out a few tit bits to the eager mouths around me I spotted 16 apparently fast asleep despite the activity of the others. On reaching her side I could see she was in fact quite dead and had probably died as I left the field earlier.

The staggers can occur after a sudden major change in diet, and I know of a farmer who after lambing his flock in a building, feeding them hay, roots and bagfood, then put them out on to some lush, heavily fertilised Italian Rye (an annual grass). In three days over three dozen of his ewes had died of magnesium deficiency, so he had a great deal of "force majeure" to report to the Ministry.

You can perhaps now see that sheep have every right to their furrowed brows and anxious cares, and I haven't yet touched on the lambs' problems!

As their shepherd I am well aware of all this and the care I need to exercise to avoid mass hysteria when I have to handle them. Even the quietest and tamest can go all to pieces and then, no matter how I try, I cannot calm them down because their faith in me has temporarily lapsed. Such paralysing fear can grip us all too easily as well, and we may have good cause if we are caught up in real danger. This happened to the disciples when that unexpected storm blew up as they were crossing the Sea of Galilee. And it must have been a very bad one, because hardened fishermen like Peter and James were terrified.

Like my sheep in moments of crisis they turned to their Shepherd and woke Jesus up; but then their fears actually heightened as He took charge of the situation. His power over the elements was even more awesome than the storm itself. He was quick to comfort and calm them, but he also chided them for their lack of trust in Him. After such a demonstration of His mighty power and His instant concern for their safety they should never have faltered in their faith in Him again - but we know that they did. And so did many men of God throughout the Old and New Testament narratives, where we can find literally hundreds of references to God telling them to "Fear not", "Be brave", "Be of good courage" etc. These certainly highlight the problem Our Father has over our very sensitive panic buttons, and our wavering trust in Him. We can so often behave as though we are facing all our difficulties and dangers alone, instead of believing Our Shepherd's promise that he *"will be with us always, even unto the end"* Matthew 28.20.

> *"Lord Jesus in fearful times give us the courage that is based on You; on Your loving and practical care of us, Your frightened sheep, and on Your Almighty Power which has triumphed over even death and the grave".*
> Amen.

AN ORFUL TIME

I had always been rather pleased with the motto I had invented for good shepherding which was: "put yourself in the sheep's place", until one unforgettable Spring, when I began to wish I'd never thought of it.

That year, we had planned to lamb in late March, rather later than usual. This was so that I could observe and record the tupping dates before I had an operation in the Autumn, and then be free of any post-operative radio-therapy treatment once lambing began.

By mid-February all seemed to have worked out well and I was planning to take things a little easier and have plenty of early nights for a month to build up my reserves. During this relatively quiet spell, as we were feeding the cattle one afternoon. I suddenly became aware of a commotion on our neighbour's field where he had brought his flock of ewes and young lambs. I could see all the sheep stampeding in terror and when we went over, we found a ewe wrapped in one of the temporary electric fence wires, and dragging the rest of the reel behind her. To the others she was like something out of a horror film and they couldn't scatter fast enough.

After alerting the neighbour, Michael went to help him disentangle the sheep and sort out the flock (some of whom actually died of fright on the spot). I continued seeing to the cattle and by the time I got round to the ewes, Michael had returned to help me and it was a great pity that he did as you will see.

A week or so after this episode I was handing out some tit-bits to the later lambers who had been separated from those who had already produced their offspring. As I gave one of my old favourite ewes a crust and fuss I noticed a strange scab on her nose. Alarm bells began ringing in my head as I peered more closely at the twenty other animals milling around me. Several of them had similar tell-tale signs. With a heavy heart I went back to the house in search of Michael.

"We've got ORF!" I told him, "it's in the flock who haven't lambed, so you'll have to feed the others and I'll keep away from them. We might contain the spread of it in that way."

"Perhaps we'll get 'orf' lightly, if we do that," quipped Michael.

We both like puns but I wasn't in the mood. My mind was concentrated on the 'orful' possibilities and how the disease had reached us. It is highly contagious, passing via clothes, shoes and handling. It can stay on hurdles for weeks, so that sheep rubbing themselves can catch it from each other. In markets, the attendants are also at risk as it is an Enzootic (transmissible to man) virus. It especially gets into cuts and grazes on one's hands.

Our sheep had not been in contact with any others, and we never go to markets, nor had we been with any other shepherds. The only source had to be our neighbour's flock and Michael must have carried it back on his boots or clothes. Of course it is also a rare but occupational hazard for shepherds to pick up such a virus too and we would have to be on the alert.

About a week later I was fascinated but hardly surprised to find a strange blister forming on the back of one of my hands. It was really quite pretty, a beautiful pink oval, about two inches long with a scalloped edge. For several days it stayed like that, while many of the ewes became very poorly. Their blisters had now spread **inside** their mouths and noses, and despite being very hungry as they were heavily pregnant they could barely eat. I gave them what soft food I could, as I was now fearing the very real possibility of pregnancy toxaemia, if they became under-nourished.

Some began to lamb in spite of their problems and everyone seemed to keep going somehow. In case my blister burst and spread elsewhere, I decided to go to the local Surgery for some antibiotic powder.

There I found myself the centre of attraction since no one in the practice had ever seen a case of "orf". I seemed to know as much about it as they did, and I certainly knew that there is no treatment for man or beast.

I had also read a gloomy article in a farming magazine which had conducted a survey amongst those farmers who had caught "orf". Many of them had resorted to homeopathy in desperation once the symptoms got worse. Some had been so depressed they had felt suicidal.

The next morning I woke to find the blister **had** burst and a rash was already spreading up my arm. Within a day both my hands and arms were covered in huge painful blisters and my fingers became so swollen that they were like bunches of bananas. Blisters soon appeared round my mouth and on my neck and legs and on top of all that I had an uncontrollable itching which increased when I was warm. Sleep was impossible and the only relief from the irritation was to plunge my arms and hands in a bucket of cold water. Somehow or other I carried on my share of the heavy farm work and the lambing with a deep, deep sympathy for my stricken ewes. I was utterly alongside them in their suffering, knowing all too well that both they and I had to face at least another week of severe symptoms, since a month seems to be the average length of an outbreak. Those 28 days seemed an eternity, but then to my amazement the itching and blisters subsided almost overnight and my hands returned to their normal size. It was like a miracle. I can still see the look of astonishment on a friend's face, as she turned my hands over and over, looking for signs of the "orf" she had seen a week before. There were virtually no scars to show for all that anguish!

Quite soon after, the ewes and I were back to our old selves. No sheep died, (young lambs with "orf" for example often stop suckling and so fade away). None had gangrene where the blisters set in and the other flock never developed the disease. We had safely come through a very trying time together.

By this sharing in the ewes' suffering albeit involuntarily, I gained a much fuller insight into their plight and their needs. In experiencing the same physical miseries, I knew how to help them better. As a result I took great pains to provide a more suitable diet instead of their normal pre-natal food. I also spent much more time talking to them and giving them love and comfort than I would otherwise have done. If you are thinking that sheep wouldn't appreciate some T.L.C. I can assure you they do!

However, if I could have chosen **not** to share in my ewes' suffering I certainly would have done so and my famous motto would have 'gone out of the window'.

Thank God that our Good Shepherd did not back out of God's plan for His sheep. He **voluntarily** came alongside us as a man, to share in our human weaknesses. He, as God, took on our vulnerability and put Himself **willingly** in our place to the uttermost, by dying in our place on the Cross. While on the earth He experienced all the intensities of human pain, sorrow, weariness, toil, rejection, and disappointment, so He knows better than we do ourselves what we are facing and what help we need, and unlike a human shepherd He has a cure for all our troubles. He offers us Himself:- *"Lo, I am with you **always**"*, and this means all His strength, serenity, endurance, peace and joy are ours for the taking.

A MINI-MIRACLE

"You are the God who does wonders" Psalm 77.14.

One of my husband's favourite sayings was.... "the impossible I can do now, miracles take a little longer"; it was his stock response to yet another D.I.Y. problem I had brought to him. Being a very able handyman I always expected him to solve anything and he never failed to rise to the occasion. Those of us who also take our God at His word know that he does wonders far beyond our imaginings, and when Jesus began His ministry He performed so many of these wonders before people's very eyes, that miracles were commonplace. But what about now?

I think many of us might hesitate and mumble something about co-incidences and chance happenings to explain anything unusual, forgetting that God uses these and indeed orders them to perform His miracles today. There will be those of you who have seen Mega-Miracles in your own lives and know of our God's wonders. But I think all of us should expect His miracles from day to day even if only on a 'mini' scale. Here on the farm I know that the sheep very often require miraculous help since they're all walking disaster areas. However, I want to tell you about an event which concerned a much more lowly creature.

It was mid-winter and at that season, much of my time is involved with fetching, shovelling up and feeding root vegetables to the stock. Between them the cattle and sheep eat roughly four tons a week, so it is quite a mammoth task. Some of the roots are grown on the farm, but parsnips which are top of the menu, and for which the cows would kill their old grannies, have to be fetched by the trailer load. I go at least once a week for a two ton load to a local Vegetable Packing centre. Here root vegetables, like carrots, turnips, and parsnips, are washed, sorted, bagged and set off to Supermarkets, while the waste (overlarge, misshapen and broken specimens) are sent out to trailers for stock feed.

On this particular day, I had gone with Don, a friend, who had volunteered to help me load; we were standing in the waste trailer, pausing for breath, after shovelling for about ten minutes or so, when he suddenly bent down and scooped up some object in his hands. To his amazement he had found a very dazed toad, one of many that hibernate in the dying tops of the roots on the fields.

"That's hardly a miracle!" I can hear you saying - "toads are common enough surely!" Yes...... **bits** of toads are, certainly - the workers in the Pack House continually see odd legs or squashed remains, passing along the belts, but never live ones. Why? Well let me explain.

This toad had been through a living hell for some hours before he fell into Don's hands and this is what will have happened......

At 7am that morning the parsnips had been lifted by a four row piece of machinery which cuts alongside the lines of roots, dragging them out of the ground. The parsnips, along with a great deal of stones, vegetation and soil then went up a fast moving belt and were hurled into a six ton trailer. Toad was too. Where he was in that load I don't know, but he was wrenched from the peace of his hibernation nest into a moving nightmare.

By 8am the load arrived at the Washer where it was backed up, raised and tipped, so that slowly but surely all the parsnips, stones, vegetation and soil and Toad tumbled down into a hopper to await their turn to be processed. Everything was then steadily taken along a moving belt to an enormous revolving drum. It is like a giant spin drier on its side, about fifteen feet long - through which gallons of water are flushing. The parsnips are washed by being tossed and turned, while the stones are separated from them; the noise is so deafening that conversation is impossible. It is a most violent and whirling affair and we can only imagine what it must be like to spin around in it.

Toad knew only too well and his ordeal wasn't over yet. Eventually, he was spewed out onto another belt which took him into the Packing Shed.

Here, he had to pass the men and women who sort and grade, and run the risk of being hurled into a rubbish bin if he'd been spotted. On he went, joining the unwanted roots up another belt to be tossed into a waste trailer. It was 11am, time for him to fall, battered but uninjured into Don's hands. If he had not done so, he would surely have been buried beneath the four ton of waste which was to fill the trailer. Why Toad had not been squashed, mangled or torn to pieces was a Miracle, culminating in him falling into safe, caring hands, so he could be put back into hibernation - this time in my greenhouse.

To us, that day, he was a living marvel, a wonderful witness to our Lord's care. If He cared for Toad like this, how much more will He care for us if we let ourselves "fall into His hands" as David did in II Samuel 24 14. David knew His Lord's mercy was great and he had seen Him perform miracles, during his lifetime.

Joshua too knew of God's wonders, as we can read in Joshua 3 for instance where the river Jordan, (a very wide and deep stretch of water) was parted so that the children of Israel could cross over. He encouraged the people by telling them *sanctify yourselves, because tomorrow the Lord will do wonders among you*" Joshua 3.5.

We may not see a mega-miracle like that each day, but let's expect at least a mini one, for "with God nothing is impossible". His power is unchanged, it is as great as in David and Joshua's times, it is only our lack of trust that hides the evidence in our lives.

MITEY MIN

You have found grace in my sight and I know you by name Exodus 33.17.

A gravelly-voiced ewe we had, called Satchmo, was never very good at maths. Knowing we liked twins, she'd duly produce a pair, but like me, sizes in ratio to one another were beyond her. Each year we'd have one fine big lamb and one thin pathetic specimen, because food supplies in the womb had been unequally shared out.

One Spring Satchmo excelled herself. She decided to lamb on the quiet while at a neighbour's field and caught me on the hop. At tea-time I found to my dismay that not only had she lambed but she had also completely prolapsed her womb. 'Emergency Ward 10' had nothing on us that day, with the vet dashing here in five minutes and the three of us stretchering Satchmo home on an old garden centre trolley. After rigging up a straw bale operating table her womb was put back into place, stitches put in and appropriate injections given. All this was accompanied by outraged bellows from the cows whose tea-time had been delayed.

Satchmo was soon up and eating and, I could fetch her lambs. Her boy was huge - 15lbs - and very hungry, but the girl was minute - 2lbs only - the size of a pack of sugar. Suckling was impossible for her and she was far too small to cope with the biting February cold. So the tiny mite had to go indoors and become our newest lodger, joining the cat and dog, both of whom philosophically accept any and each newcomer.

After two days she managed to stand and was all of six inches tall! She then began to bleat in a thin reedy voice - reminiscent of 'Min' of the old Goon Shows on the radio, and so she just had to be called 'Mitey Min'. Once she was on her feet she took us over. She was the first in the food queue, first in front of the open fire - fascinated by the flames, and first on walks up the lane with Michael, the dog and cat. The sight of this procession brought any traffic to an amazed halt.

She was always the centre of attraction with young and old, who vied with each other to bottle feed her, entertaining us all as she gambolled about indoors or out in the garden, where, as we worked, she grazed alongside us. After two months she was big enough not to squeeze out of the sheep netting and could be put in with some of our other sheep. Obviously over this time she became totally tame, house-trained, knew commands, and her name. She was much easier to train than a dog.

Ten years later and with several lamb crops of her own, Mitey Min is a large placid independent ewe. But she is as tame as ever, comes when she is called and will shoot indoors if she ever gets onto the garden. She can then be found in the dining room chewing the telephone wire, which she adored as a baby.

Now, although I know all my ewes as individuals, in Mitey Min's case **I know her by name**, which is very special. Indeed, I know her so well that I can anticipate her reactions to most situations, and when I think of my sheep it is Mitey Min I picture first - it is she who will always follow me even if the rest of the flock refuse to do so.

Psalm 139 tells us how God knows us - verses 1 to 6, "All of us are individually loved and known", (it's all too wonderful and I can hardly take it in). As our Lord said - Matthew chapter 10 verse 30 - *"even the hairs on our heads are numbered"*. In Psalm 139 verses 17 and 18 we read - *"His thoughts towards us are more in number than the sand"*. And He knows us by name as He did Moses.

And just think what happened to Zaccheus, Luke Chapter 19 verse 5, Jesus knew his name (they did not have to be introduced); Jesus called out to him by name, - not "Hey you! Up in the tree", but **Zaccheus**! Come down....".

When Jesus calls us, will we eagerly do his bidding like 'Mitey Min' does mine and like Zaccheus did that day?

SIDNEY

If you had the misfortune to be as well-acquainted with Sidney as I am, the word 'bashful' would take on a whole new meaning. He has one way of dealing with everything he meets in life - it is.... "thump it first and ask questions later". If a gate is in his way, he smashes it up, and the same goes for hurdles. If he doesn't like the tea on offer he hurls bucket and all into the air. If he doesn't fancy his hay, he even sets about the hay net! If he wants to rejoin his wives and I am trying to keep him out of the sheep house, he attacks the walls and doors. Station Farm has often rung to the sound of his repeated butting of corrugated iron. It is guaranteed to bring on an instant headache, in me of course, not him - no, I think **his** head is full of concrete. To Sidney nothing is sacred, but it would not be quite so bad if he only focused his anger on inanimate objects. Sadly, for all us farm inhabitants, no one is safe from attack. He is no respecter of persons, and that even includes the cows. When he was once put with Emma, an 8cwt Dexter and her brawny son so he would have some company while the ewes lambed, he so terrorised them that they could not even get to their food! His attitude to his wives

is not much kinder - he believes it is "Rams first, women and children last", especially at teatime. He really is a complete "male chauvinist", and when his ewes are not ready to welcome his attentions, he steps back

and then charges, hitting them amidships until they give him the respect he thinks he is owed.

He became a father when only a year old (sheep are very precocious) and on spotting his firstborn children, a pair of premature twins, which lay helplessly awaiting my ministrations, he butted one so hard it was hurled across the building into the wall. It was never quite the same again. He must have thought such weaklings did not fit his virile image and found them a disappointment. So did I for that matter, but they needed some T.L.C., not shaking up. Since then, he has always had to be kept away from his young, at least until they are up and running. Don't think, by the way, after reading this that he is unhandleable - on the contrary, he comes when he is called, rather too headlong for comfort; knows his name, and loves a fuss. This is, of course, very deceptive when visitors first meet him, and when they are told of his exploits they are always sure I am giving him a bad press. Until, that is, they relax their guard and unwisely go into his field.

Everyone is somehow attracted to him, because he is certainly a fine figure of a ram. He has the broad handsome black head of a Suffolk sheep, huge handlebar ears, strong sturdy black legs, and a soft white fleece. Being 250 lbs in weight, and most of that muscle, has meant that he has produced magnificent lambs in large quantities, since with his virility not even a china ewe is safe. He also feels that I really ought to be part of his harem and takes me completely for granted; but I will come to his cavalier treatment of the hand that feeds him a bit later.

On the rare occasions that he has been ill 'butter wouldn't melt in his mouth'. He is only too glad of any help and this was especially so when during his second summer with me, he became severely dehydrated during a very hot spell of weather. Stones formed in his urethra and for five days he was obviously in agony, and not even pain-killers, which were so strong they are given to horses, helped him. I massaged and bathed him and during all this care he was as meek as one of his own lambs.

Eventually the Vet and I reluctantly decided he must be put out of his misery: but Sidney must have overheard the telephone conversation because by the time I had gone out to say 'goodbye' to him, he had rallied and was able to relieve himself at last. Two days later he was back to his old self - in other words he was chasing after me with malice aforethought. There is no denying he is a 'tough cookie' and is short on gratitude and temper, as one winter's afternoon proved.

This time it was me who was poorly, and I was having to carry on the farm work when I should have been in bed. Sidney was unfortunately the last to be fed and quite unsympathetic to my state. He was very impatient over such slow waitress service and angry with the basic menu of roots and hay. Where was the nice man who had helped feed him the day before and had given him all those extra tit bits? If I wasn't going to produce some, then he, Sidney, was going to find some for himself. But first of all, he would give his useless Shepherd a good bashing up. I realised his intent as I went back into the field bearing the hay for him and a couple of cattle. Those rolling eyes, showing all the whites, and the ears back meant Sidney was about to charge. I really felt too feeble for such an attack, but I had got to face him somehow. Dropping the hay, I grabbed the muck fork which was handy and shouted a warning. This made him even more furious and be began pinning me to the Cow Shed wall, despite being prodded by the sharp prongs. Steel, my Alsatian, who was then only a youngster, tried to come to my rescue as I yelled for help. Sidney turned to give him a terrible blow in the ribs, so quite naturally he retired hurt, although obviously upset that I was still in danger. I really felt that Sidney would have liked to kill me, for I have never seen a ram so violent and determined as he was that day, and I have dealt with several over the years. Even four month old ram lambs will come up and give you a good biff.

It is good spectator sport but it is not so funny for the one on the receiving end I can tell you! Rams have been known to kill farmers and should **never** be under-estimated. At the least an unexpected blow to one's legs could cause a bad fall and even a break, while lurid bruising is commonplace.

Just recently I have decided I must cut down my work load and phase out the sheep. Many of the ewes are elderly and are to be given honourable retirement and they will end their days on the Farm. Sidney must either accept voluntary redundancy or be sold on. His belligerence would constantly threaten mine and the ewes' peace, so there really is no choice for him. He may find his new home does not come up to his standards, so I expect he will renew his battles with his new owner.

Sidney's constant fight against my control reminds me so much of mankind's natural reaction to God's claim on their lives. It seems instinctive in us to resent and reject a Creator being who because He made us does have rights to our allegiance. Paul says this plainly enough in Romans 8.7. that 'man's mind is naturally hostile to God'. This hostility reached a peak when men, particularly 'righteous' Jews, met God's son. These reasoning and reasonable men (not thick-headed rams, who would know no better) killed God! Perhaps had 20th Century men faced Jesus they might have been less barbaric, preferring to believe scientific 'truth', (in the evolution theory, for example, there is no place for a Creator), so scornful laughter and complete indifference might have replaced the Cross. But of course, Jesus' death and resurrection was God's rescue plan for those of us who give up our fight against Him. This is when the Peace Treaty between us and Our God is signed, and the "perfect peace of a mind stayed on God" becomes ours.

That should be an end to our fighting, but like Sidney we still can't help beating our heads against the wall. I know I have found "Your will be done" a very hard prayer during hard times. I have had to ask my Shepherd's help to avoid the angry resentment, which is all too near the surface, welling up in me. But as I am now on His side, I have all His weapons and defence against such times. He has promised to be with me always, through everything and be "my shield and my defender".

What a contrast to what happened to the Assyrians when their mighty army went up against Jerusalem. Their hatred and scorn of God had brought them into a one-sided match. They took on Almighty Jehovah and lost - in such a big way, that 185,000 picked fighting men died overnight - slain by an Angel. They hadn't realised what Paul knew when he wrote "if God is for us, who can be against us?" Romans 8.31. Puny, insignificant man against the Omnipotent Creator? Even Sidney wouldn't join in that fight, I'm sure.

SNOOPY

"If a man has a hundred sheep and one wanders away, will he not leave the ninety and nine and seek the one that is lost"? Matthew 18.

It was typical lambing weather, cold, drizzly, with a keen east wind blowing; so I wasn't surprised to find N°· 20 had decided to choose this day. As I huddled in the near-by wood, keeping watch over her, the first lamb quickly arrived. It was very small and since she had become quite  enormous. I guessed there might be two more to come. Baby was licked for a while, then Mother lay down to produce the other lambs, leaving Tiny shivering in the wind and rain. Once all three lambs had safely arrived I could gather them up and lead '20' back to the shelter of the Sheep House. By this time Snoopy as I had christened little-un was beginning to suffer from hypothermia. This is a disastrous drop in body temperature which quickly affects small lambs and soon kills them.

I penned up '20' and family, then set up the warming box beside her and laid Snoopy in it. This box is a wonderful device which my husband made; it consist of a tiny fan heater built into a flameproof frame where the lamb can be warmed up without being separated from the ewe. She can still see him and lick and love him during those first hours of life when the vital bond between them is established. A separation at this time, even if only for an hour, can result in the ewe rejecting her baby, as we had found to our cost in the past.

I then milked '20', getting about 6oz of precious colostrum out for Snoopy so I could give him a couple of feeds via a stomach tube whilst he was weakly. By tea-time all three lambs and '20' seemed well, but seeing that Snoopy's bond with his mother was rather poor, I decided to feed him again at bed-time and then somewhere in the middle of the night. 3am found me groping my way down to the Sheep House with a bottle of warm milk at the ready. I checked first on three other new sheep families and finally reached '20's pen. Being short of space, I had put her beside the tattered door that led into the Cow's yard. I had blocked the gaps at the bottom with a straw bale in case tiny Snoopy might try to squeeze out. When I peered into the pen he was nowhere to be seen. "Where's your baby?" I asked '20'. Now if a sheep could shrug its shoulders, that is what '20' did; then she nudged her two big boys who were snuggled together, as if to say "I've got these two and I'm quite happy."

I rushed into the main part of the Sheep House and asked the other ewes if they had seen Snoopy. I searched everywhere including the cow yard, even wondering if a cow had trodden him into the mud. I HAD to find Snoopy! If he was outside he'd have hypothermia again as it was cold and pouring with rain and by daylight he would most certainly be dead. Then I did what I should have done at the beginning - I asked God to help me find him. Now I felt sure he was in the cow yard so I sploshed back into it, my torch fading fast. This time I noticed that a rather daft bullock we had at that stage was staring pop-eyed at something in the middle of the yard. I followed his gaze and there was Snoopy! He was quietly trying to drown in a cow's footprint! Scooping him up, I rushed back to the House.

Here in the light I could see he was soaked, covered in mud and close to death. Putting him in the washing up bowl, I gently bathed him in warm water. He didn't respond, but remained completely floppy. Then I laid him down and towelled him. Still no response. After that, I placed him in front of a fan heater for a while. Still no response! So I turned to my last resort. Opening the Rayburn oven, I laid him inside on an old towel. Half an hour later he began to lift his head and I could feed him a little warmed milk. By 4.30am I felt it was safe to leave him in a cardboard box beside the open oven and I could go back to bed.

Next morning, he was bleating and up and about and he never looked back. Of course, '20' would not accept him again, so he had to be bottle reared, and grew into a fine tame ram. So I could "rejoice" as Our Lord does, "over one sheep in a hundred that was lost and is found, not wanting any to perish". God's love for us is so great that He patiently seeks us out and draws us back to Himself even when we rebuff His advances and do not respond. He is not content to wait until we return to His fold, but searches for us, no matter what it costs Him, as demonstrated on the Cross.

THE BREAK OUT

Everyone to his own way Isaiah 53.6.

Unlike sheep, cattle have a very cavalier attitude towards their home and their herdsman (or woman, in my case). They are no respecters of persons, they have a great 'joie de vivre' and even matronly cows can behave like very naughty children who are particularly fond of practical jokes. So, they certainly do not take life over-seriously, are not so easily panicked as sheep and have an over-developed sense of curiosity. They also have insatiable appetites, and are really walking stomachs (remember each cow has 4 apiece, with the largest being over a quarter of their body mass). Most weigh over half a ton too.

Put all these factors together, add a break-out, and you have a recipe for disaster! Neighbouring land, gardens, crops and property are all fair game to a rampaging herd who will only return home when **they** feel like it! Naturally, we have always been very aware of this and daily check our cattle's fencing, especially trying to make sure their electric fence is giving a good shock, should they try to test the defences. Above all an ample food supply must be constantly available be it grazing or winter fodder, if not, the cows are liable to take the law into their own hands (or rather hooves) and go in search of something to eat.

Occasionally, one or two animals have escaped, usually a small calf who has squeezed through the wires with an anxious mother in tow. That has been a nuisance, but not a great problem. So, with fifteen relatively peaceful years as a cowgirl behind me, I was quite unprepared for **THE COW EVENT** of last year.

It was a beautiful March morning showing much promise of Spring - the cows were quietly breakfasting on their winter 'sacrifice' field and the birds were singing their hearts out as a friend and I began some fencing repairs. An excited moo suddenly burst forth shattering the peace; it was quickly followed by many others, replying to the first. Knowing each cow's voice and their intonations, I knew it all meant TROUBLE - for me anyway.

The two of us rushed across to the farm to be met by a chaotic scene. Somehow or other the electric fence had been brought down and the bolder members of the herd were already out and racing off in all directions. A few young calves and their more elderly and cautious mothers were still dithering at the fallen wires. We had to do something quickly, if we were going to round everyone up. Fighting rising hysteria, I sent my friend around the buildings in the hope of heading them off while I grabbed a plastic sack and put some roots in it and rattled it temptingly, calling to individuals who know their names. Our efforts had no effect whatever - if anything everyone became even more excited and a grand steeplechase began through my wood. Fallen trees were leaped, as udders swung crazily, some bullocks took to fighting and the whole herd charged back and forth sweeping us aside. Despite the dangers, no one injured themselves and eventually all ended up on the little field of the neighbouring holiday cottage, where they had found some GRASS AT LAST! I could see that they would never be persuaded back to their winter quarters, so my long-suffering friend (who had never actually met cattle before that day) and I put up a temporary fence around them and hoped the cottage owners would not pay an unexpected visit. From then on, I had to let the cattle out on to their proper grazing, a month earlier than I had intended, and bring them in at nights until the grass really started to grow.

I wonder if we have ever hindered God's plans and caused chaos like this? Of course, our mighty Father can overrule our actions and use other means, but that does not excuse us when we exercise self-will. Paul was concerned that his actions should not "*hinder the gospel of Christ*" 1 Corinthians 9.12. and in the previous chapter he warns us to "take heed unless our liberty becomes a stumbling block" to others. Our responsibility for our fellows is very great and so our actions must be taken in the light of this.

Before we became Christ's, we were like "everyone who has gone his own way" heedless of our Creator's claims on us. We were absorbed in ourselves, just like my cows are, but unlike them "*we shall be called to account for our actions*" Romans 14.12.

> *Thy way not mine O Lord,*
> *However dark it be,*
> *Lead me by thine own hand,*
> *Choose out the path for me.*   Hymns Ancient & Modern No. 356

R N E D

"Your rod and staff comfort me".

The Roman Nose ewe's daughter had won the lambing prize in the spring, having produced an amazingly strong family of **Quads**! Triplets are quite common amongst my flocks but this was a first for her and me. She needed a little help to feed them for a month or so, especially bearing in mind that ewes only have 2 teats. But after that she reared them alone and they were soon competing in size with other lambs who were only twins. To produce sufficient milk, she needed high-quality grazing and plenty of it - no wonder she was always hungry that year. However, she is a good doer and by the time the lambs were weaned and we were a month away from tupping time again, her body condition was quite good. To make sure she would have plenty of reserves for another good conception, I put her and the rest of the flock on some fresh, rich pasture which had grown very well after a cut of hay. This is known as 'flushing' - i.e. building up the ewe well, so that when she takes the ram she will have a multiple ovulation.

Unfortunately, a warm and rainy spell followed, and the grazing became not only lush but very wet, spelling disaster for such a greedy feeder as R N E D. Since it was early September, flies were still abundant on warm and muggy days, with the dreaded greenbottles especially numerous. So I was not surprised to find a very unhappy ewe on one of my visits to the flock. R N E D was pecking at the grass, then turning to stare at her rear end. She was holding herself in a strange twisted way and all the time her tail was waggling back and forth. To a shepherd one or all of these signs spell out just one thing - FLY STRIKE.

This condition is the stuff of science fiction - I am sure a Hitchcock film could have made a real horror story out of it. If the thought of maggots makes your flesh creep, just picture a ewe's plight. She has perhaps soiled her fleece around her tail (as R N E D had) and the resultant smell attracts all the greenbottles in the district. They eagerly lay hundreds of their eggs on her back and if the temperature is high enough, in twelve hours tiny thread-like maggots will hatch. They start to feed on her oily wool, by secreting a fluid which breaks the material down so that they can absorb the oozy waste. They grow at an amazing speed and are soon through to her flesh which they attack in the same way. Within days large areas of raw and gaping wounds cover her body and the putrid smell attracts both blue and greenbottles who all come to add their eggs, so that she is soon host to thousands of maggots. She is literally being eaten alive and as if this is not enough, the larvae produce toxins which pass into the sheep's bloodstream and these can kill particularly susceptible animals like young lambs.

Like us humans some sheep are more stoic than others - I have had a lamb die from a strike no bigger than a coin, I have had ewes demented and depressed by a handful of maggots, while I have seen one lamb (not under my care I hasten to add) who had half his body affected, but who still survived.

Well, to get back to R N E D - rather than gather all the flock into a building in order to catch her, I decided to treat her there on the field. I felt sure her great appetite and tameness might allow me to entice her to the gate. I made up a solution of dip and put it in a 2 litre bottle, and also armed myself with a halter and some tasty titbits. I waved these about as I called and sure enough R N E D led the rush to have a share out. Once she was engrossed I slipped the rope round her and quickly tied her up. I could then dag (clip) her rear-end and expose the maggot-ridden patches onto which I poured the dip which quickly flushed out the larvae, and would also protect her from further attacks. By evening, R N E D was her usual cheerful self and was ready for me to make a fuss of her. She had happily accepted my 'rod' of handling, knowing the discipline would be of benefit. My 'rod' (a rope instead of a shepherd's crook) had brought her comfort which she could never have found herself.

Our Father has adopted us as His children, once we have accepted Christ as His son, and like an earthly father He needs to discipline us. So we must not "lose heart when He rebukes us, because He disciplines those he loves". We want His fatherly love and care but don't always want to endure His Rod. But His way is always best, He knows what is right for us, even though it may not make sense or seem fair to us at the time. We cannot necessarily understand WHY Our Lord puts us under His Rod, any more than R N E D knew why I was tying her up. But let us not "lose heart" but trust and accept His work in us, just as she gave in to my handling.

ENA SHARPLES

Even to your old age I am He, and to grey hair I will carry you. I have made and I will bear, I will carry and I will save Isaiah 46.4.

Those wonderful words from Isaiah came home to me very strongly recently, as I was forced to make a decision over an old ewe in my flock. She had certainly reached her old age, being well into her teens and with many grey hairs around her muzzle. Ena Sharples, as we called our little back ewe, (owing to her tattered ears and curly head), joined our flock at about 8 years old, when we bought several ewe lambs including her daughters. Since then, she has given us another seven years of loyal service, but if she had been part of a large Farm's flock, this would not have happened. Under the management of these estates, the ewes are usually culled after about five lamb crops, because, beyond this age, pregnancy and metabolic disorders increase and the profit margin will not carry any weakness of the sheep. There can be no mercy, so that the ewes do not find that 'goodness and mercy follow them all the days of their lives'.

Ena needed much compassion because like us she had her failings. Perhaps her greatest was due to her size - she was very small and generally could not lamb by herself. She could never produce more than one leg, or a head, or just a tail and would leave me to sort out the rest and deliver the lambs. Through seven lambings I had to save her and the babies from certain death, but she was quick to realise where to turn to for help. She had the good sense to bleat loudly for assistance, just as Our Lord wants us to turn to Him, as we find in Psalm 55 verse 17 *"Evening, morning and at noon I will pray and cry aloud and He shall hear my voice"*. Ena's favourite time to cry aloud was 3am (a popular lambing time) and she never failed to wake me up! Her joy and mine were full when we had produced two strong lambs which she always fed so well they were soon bigger than herself. She guarded them fiercely and was a marvellous mother, making full use of her talents like the "good and faithful servant" in Jesus' parable in Matthew 25.

As time went on, I had to carry Ena through the problems of her older years, particularly as she lost her teeth and could not compete with the other ewes. Finally, she had to be carried home, out of the flock, because she was ill. We gently bore her back as lovingly as Our Shepherd does us, and to-day I made the painful decision to give her a merciful end in my arms. As I said 'Goodbye' to her, I thought of how God has been faithful to His promise "He has made and He has borne" with us in all our failings and faithlessness. I know I let Him down far more than Ena Sharples ever failed me, and yet "He has carried me" through everything and especially close in His arms during Michael's terminal illness. My love and patience with my old ewe are but pale shadows of His goodness and mercy to us - the greatest Shepherd of them all!

ABANDONED AND ADOPTED

1. PERKY

Lambing had been quite a struggle for Mitey Min; she had finally produced two large lambs who had taken their time to come into the world. In fact, the second was born two hours after the first, which is unusual, the interval is normally much less than an hour. So it was no wonder the ewe was tired; she was also rather grumpy and when I  returned to see how things were, she turned to her ewe lamb (the second born) and knocked her out of the way. My heart sank. Was she rejecting the baby? As I continued to watch, it was plain that she had taken a dislike to the lamb. Goodness knows why! It was a lively and sturdy infant with as much charm as its brother as far as I could see. I tried to encourage baby to suck but Mum would have none of it. Ruefully, I milked some of Mitey Min's colostrum and gave the now very hungry infant a bottle. I left the family complete for an hour or so longer, but I could see that Perky (it seemed a good name for such a bright youngster) was being repeatedly butted and would come to harm if left in the pen with mother.

So yet another 'orphan' joined the 'lamb pool'. Such out and out abandonment is not common in sheep, in fact, over the years I have only known it to happen twice and in both cases the lambs were strong and healthy, so it was inexplicable. Most ewes will stick by the most sickly and hopeless of infants until death intervenes and even then they will bleat and search for their lost baby for some days. It seems to me that we humans are much less caring as parents than sheep, because abortions, child abuse and abandoned babies are run of the mill today.

In Isaiah 49.15, we can find the same thoughts *"Can a mother forget the baby at her breast and have no compassion on the child she has borne?"* and of course, sadly, the answer is 'Yes'. But God then gives us a wonderful promise. The verse continues: *"Though she may forget, I will not forget you! See I have engraved you on the palms of my hands...."*. If, like me, you have often written a memo for yourself on your hand, you will appreciate this picture. But God's words are stronger than this, because He has ETCHED us on His hands, never to be removed. We are His for Eternity.

2. N°· 14

N°· 09 had done it again! She had lambed at about 5am, a week early and given me no warnings, as usual, and this time she had made a real mess of things. She had had just one baby and it was enormous. It was also very dead and must have taken a great deal of effort to produce. It had probably come out with one leg back, if not both front limbs tucked back. Why ever hadn't she bleated for help? I slept close by the lambing shed and always heard the ewes' calls. There was nothing I could do for her lamb, but as she was a very good mother with a milky udder, I felt that it might be worth trying to give her a foster child. However, as I didn't have any orphan lambs at that point I rang round my neighbouring farmers to see if they could find one. Eventually, I located a suitable lamb and set off to pick it up. It was certainly a fine strong ram lamb, but it was at least a fortnight old and I doubted if '09' would accept one of this age...

As I drove home, I decided that I had better skin her dead baby and put its coat on N°· 14 (the number the orphan bore on his side). I have to admit that I had never tackled such a task before, although I had seen it done.

I cannot claim to have made a very professional job of it and the area where I performed the operation looked as though I had committed a particularly messy murder; still, I now had a new coat for '14', which I tied round his tum, put his legs through the holes and made sure the tail was over his (this is essential because mother sniffs her baby very carefully in this department). So '14' should smell as well as look like '09' own lamb; hoping this would do the trick I tentatively introduced N°· 14 to '09'. To my huge relief and amazement, they loved one another on sight and '14' dived under Mum for a good breakfast, while she checked him all over. After that, the pair were inseparable and '09' regarded him as her very own lamb. In his borrowed skin he was right in '09's sight and he became her adopted son.

This parallels our relationship with Our Father, for if we have accepted Christ as our Saviour, we have "*put on the Lord Jesus Christ*" Romans 13.14 and "*if we are clothed in His righteousness*" we are right with God and can become His adopted children. Then we can cry "*Abba, Father*" Gal. 4.6 and we can take our place in His family.

MAY

"He has blotted out the handwriting of laws that was against us, which was contrary to us and took it out of the way, nailing it to His Cross.....

Colossians 2.14.

Florushdon of Knotting (May for short) was born 10 years ago, when the May was blooming. A month premature, she weighed in at only 30lbs, but would top the scales at 9cwt now, because May is a pedigree Dexter cow. This means that her birth was registered in the annual Herd Book, where all her calvings are also recorded. She and her cousin Cherry were small enough as babes to be brought to Norfolk in the back of a Land Rover and went to live with Nigel, who bucket reared them and thoroughly spoiled them. They had all the best food in vast quantities, so it is no wonder that May grew. She also grew to be extremely naughty and wilful, because if Dexters are allowed to get away with things they are intelligent enough to twist you round their little hooves!

Once May became a winsome heifer and began to look for a husband, trouble started. Nigel was not good at fencing, so I was soon receiving frantic phone calls telling me that she and Cherry had escaped again. Being 40 miles distant, all I could do was to urge him to go and find them quickly before they caused an accident. They were usually to be found stomping along the main road to Norwich - off to do some shopping and see the bright lights I suppose! When both May and Cherry produced a fine son apiece, these turned out to be even naughtier than their mothers and Nigel could not cope. In desperation, he shut them up in his garage and asked me if I would take them and with some misgivings I agreed.

Soon after their arrival, they earned themselves the nickname of the Loonies because their behaviour turned the farm into a madhouse. They escaped, breaking most of the fences, despite the fact that they were electrified; they fought all my other cattle, vandalised the cowshed and got quite out of hand. So the four of them had to be separated, penned up and sorted out. They all had to be disciplined, but especially May, who was definitely the ringleader. Haltering, the teaching of verbal commands (above all "NO"!), and getting May used to hand milking (because she had calved again with far too much milk for her new daughter) all took time. For three weeks she kicked and knocked me about, until one day she suddenly gave in and settled down to enjoy her special treat of goodies and revel in all the fuss and love we gave her and became very affectionate in return.

Like May we will need to be chastened and disciplined and even broken to God's yoke so that we can take our place in His family and yield ourselves to His will, as she has to mine. Now she is much more content in the security of her new home and herd, and continues to give me loyal service. Sadly, I had to part with her cousin because I could not get her in calf again and I can only guess at her fate. It is a hard fact of farming life that sometimes you have quite literally to pass a death sentence on unprofitable animals however much you love them because they fail to reach your standards.

How do we stand in relation to God's standards? Let us carefully consider Jesus's summary of them and see. We are asked to "love the Lord our God with ALL our heart and our neighbours as we do ourselves". An impossible ideal; we certainly love ourselves - we can't help it, but it is difficult to love our family like that, let alone our fellows. And who can say they love God with the devotion and utter obedience which would result from loving Him with every scrap of our being? So measured against God's commandments we all fail. Perhaps you are thinking 'so what?' Well, sentence has been passed on us, we have condemned ourselves and Romans 23 tells us "The wages of sin (i.e. our failure to keep God's laws) is death". The one certain fact for all of us is that we will die - there is no need to ask a fortune teller about that! But God in His great love has provided a way for us to escape out of this, He has bailed us out - look at Colossians 2.14: "He has blotted out the evidence", wiped it away, like those shiny calendars where you can wipe off your notes and re-write something. And that is not all, God has done far more than this, He has taken the sentence with our names on it and nailed it to Jesus's cross (above every cross the crime was written up for all to see). So Jesus paid the price of our sentence by dying in our stead. This means we can have victory over death, over evil, over our failings and have Eternal Life. "Love so amazing as this demands our all" - our hearts, minds and wills in service to Him; in our gratitude we will long to please and obey Him.

May, if you remember, has her name in the Dexter Herd Book, unlike her cousin, and her future is secure, her earlier disobedience and failings forgotten. She is even trustworthy enough to be taken out on trips to help me tell her story. The Bible also talks of the Lamb's Book of Life (Rev. 21.27). There we read that those who have accepted Him as Lord of their lives have their names recorded. Before you put this down, picture that Cross with your name and sentence above it. Have you thanked Him for that sacrifice, is your name in the Book of Life, your Eternal future secure?

THE LAMBING

"How shall I give you up?..... My heart recoils within me, my compassion grows warm and tender for I am God not man" Hosea 11.8.

Lambing was well under way and this looked like a routine evening with two or three ewes promising to produce their young very shortly. I planned to make hourly visits to the Sheep House once I had made a meal for us. Sure enough, by 8pm. two shearlings were vying with each other for my attention. One was a great favourite of mine, Tripper 1 Shear, who loved being tickled under her arms and was happy to have me in attendance. The other was Tiny 2's daughter, who, from being quiet and affectionate, had become the most nervous and scattiest of all the ewes. Just recently, in a fit of panic, she had tried to jump over the large metal hay feeder; failing miserably to clear it, she had become straddled on top, needing urgent rescue. Quite expecting her to abort her lambs after all that silliness, I was pleased that she had gone full term. Now, as I sat with Tripper, I could see that all was not well with 'Daft Head' as my husband had dubbed her.

She would lie down, strain, get up, pace off, dig up the floor, get down again, strain, look worried, get up and sniff the straw in the hopes that baby had popped out unawares, and then be off again. Nothing was appearing when she strained - I was hoping to see a tiny hoof waving at me, or better still two, but after an hour of this there was no progress. Tripper's happy event was further away, so I left her and quietly tried to steal up on the other Shearling as she lay down and was absorbed and distracted. But it was hopeless; every movement I made got her up and I had not the slightest chance of catching her. A little later, I began to see a big nose starting to poke out when she made an especially great effort. Action on my part was needed! She would never give birth without at least one leg to keep that head company. I **had** to corner her, so I would have to get reinforcements.

Returning with Michael, we set about trying to creep up on her from two sides, but it was even more hopeless and our activities were upsetting and frightening the other 50 or so ewes, who were all heavily pregnant. Losing patience, Michael went away saying she deserved to cope on her own and I knew just how he felt. But as I watched her ever increasing exhaustion, I knew that the lamb would soon be dead - its head and tongue were swelling to enormous proportions - and mother was in danger as well. "How could I give her up"? Praying for a chance to catch hold of her, I went back into the ewes' midst; I decided to kneel down (not in a fit of excessive piety, but so as to be as inconspicuous as possible). Then, at each strain, while she was occupied, I inched nearer her on my hands and knees - very painful it was too, because the floor is uneven and stony. After what seemed like hours, I was almost behind her! I launched myself into a flying tackle and I had her! Somehow I hung on, even though she weighs far more than me, and once I'd regained my breath I frogmarched her to the front of the building, shoved her into a pen, slammed the hurdle shut and leaned heavily on it to recover. Now I needed Michael again to hold her still, and a bucket of disinfectant and my Slip Jel so that I could start work.

On examination, I found that the head was far too swollen to be pushed back, but I managed to reach one leg. This I gently hooked out to join the nose; during the struggle, Baby was eyeing me balefully, as if to say 'Whatever are you messing about at? Get me out of here quickly'. Well, now I could try pulling when Mum strained and slowly, we inched out one of the biggest lambs I have ever seen. Baby was poorly but alive and Mother seemed to have taken no harm and happily started licking and cleaning her lamb. Then I checked that there were no more lambs inside her, and as I was groping about I touched something slimy and knobbly. On drawing it out, we could see it was the remains of a long dead lamb, so this explained why there had been only one big single.

Daft Head and Junior were soon on their feet, him sucking his fill of warm milk and she nibbling some hay. Looking at them I felt a surge of joy and awe that always comes with every birth on the farm, whether it is lamb, calf or chick. It is all so perfect - no wonder our God was so pleased with His work of Creation and saw that "It was very good" - a typical Bible understatement! He was especially seeing this in Man, the pinnacle of His Creation. And yet He knew we would defile, pollute, exploit and devastate His handiwork, both in our own bodies and in the world at large. But he has not given up on us and wiped us off the face of His earth as we deserve. Instead, "His compassion grew so warm and tender", that He gave up His own Son to save this fallen world and that means me and you, if we believe on Jesus and His redeeming work on the Cross. And still, His compassion does not stop there; He is continually drawing us closer to Him, even, thank goodness, when we turn away from Him. He will not let us go, He cannot leave His work unfinished in us and like that lambing, He takes hold of us, even when we are rejecting His help or guidance.

The more we think we can manage and are self-sufficient, the more He will break us down, until we realise that we must depend on Him and our "sufficiency must be of God". What He wants of us, is our wholehearted willingness to be His alone and "to do His Will" not ours. He wants us to trust and obey like Tripper 1 Shear does me, instead of fighting His plans like Tiny 2's daughter fought mine. If Tripper believes I know best, how much more should we believe that of or wonderful, caring Lord - "surely His goodness and mercy will follow me all the days of my life".

THE MIX-UP

For the eyes of the Lord run to and fro throughout the whole earth on behalf of those whose heart is blameless towards him 2 Chronicles 16.9.

At lambing time it is necessary to make regular checks day and night, to see if any ewe is about to lamb. This is despite carefully recording every individual sheep's tupping day in the autumn. As the gestation is normally 147-150 days you can have a good idea of lambing dates. However, any ewe who is carrying big twins or triplets is liable to produce them up to ten days early. And like us humans the happy event can occur at any time of the day or night.

So, just as Our Lord watches over us, my eyes need to be running to and fro throughout the fields and sheep house on their behalf. Of course, some ewes announce their intention to lamb several hours before - bleating in a special way, refusing to run-

out with the rest of the flock, digging nests, hiding in a corner, going off alone and so-on.

On this particular morning I knew I had two sheep due - N°· 16 and the Roman Nose Ewe. Both were showing signs of restlessness the night before, so I expected to see something happening on my 6am visit. Nevertheless, I did not quite expect what I found. There at the back of the building were the pair of them, very close together, surrounded by a crowd of babies with the Roman Nose Ewe producing a large black lamb when I arrived.

I scratched my head in amazement - there were four lambs gathered around N°· 16, another was on its own and the newest arrival was being licked by the Roman Nose Ewe. All the lambs were still very wet and must have come along together, and N°· 16 was insisting she had quads at the very least.

Now none of my ewes had ever had quads, so I did not believe her. She and the Roman Nose Ewe had often had three, so I decided that they both had triplets. But which lambs belonged to which ewe? Both sheep were black and of the lambs, 5 were black and the 6th was speckled. Over the years N°· 16 has only ever had black lambs, so she had to have three of the four that stood round her. The last black lamb to arrive was definitely from the Roman Nose Ewe and as she had whitish lambs before, the speckled one had to be hers. So all I had to do was to pick her out one of the bunch of four black lambs.

I chose the biggest and put it aside, picked up the three smallest for N°· 16, (as she is a much smaller ewe) and set off with her following me. I penned her and her family up, so as to establish the vital bond between mother and children. I then returned for the Roman Nose Ewe and gathered up the remaining lambs and penned that group as well.

After giving the cows and all the rest of the sheep and lambs breakfast I went back to see how the two new families were doing. I could see at once that there was trouble! N°· 16 would not let any of the lambs suckle, and time was running out for the babies to get the essential early colostrum - no later than four hours after birth, preferably ages before that.

I turned to the Roman Nose Ewe and found that she was butting one of her lambs away... it was surely too big for 16, but perhaps I had made a mistake... I decided I must have mixed the lambs up, so I took away the rejected baby and gave it to 16 who immediately fussed over it.

Now I had to choose the right one to take away from N°· 16! As far as I can remember I picked one with a pin, but the Roman Nose Ewe said I had made the right choice and all was well at last with both families.

These two ewes had quite definitely "Known their lambs and were known of them" John 10.14. In spite of my inept interference. How wonderful it is for us to know that our Great Shepherd knows us and "None shall pluck us from his hand". John 10.29. So we are safe in His care no matter what happens to us.

He will also open our eyes to see his truth, just as my eyes were opened over the mix-up. And He will open our eyes to understand his word, as David prayed in Psalm 119.18.

THE EYES HAVE IT

Our eyes wait upon the Lord Psalm 123.2.

David's comparison of those who keep their eyes fixed on their Lord to a servant watching his master - never taking his eyes off him, so that he can instantly and joyfully obey his master's every wish and continually please him, reminds me of two very contrasting ewes I have owned. Both always fastened their eyes on me the moment I entered their field, but for very different reasons. Their behaviour mirrors ours towards our Lord and has given me a little insight into His joy and sadness and longings over our various responses to His wishes.

'Crazy Annie' as my husband called her, was a large black ewe with a weird, white patch on one half of her face. She was a shepherd's nightmare, being exceedingly nervous, with a very sensitive panic button. (All sheep share this trait, but in Crazy Annie's case it went to ridiculous extremes). She was terrified if you actually met her gaze, since she was looking at you in fear, ready to run if you so much as stepped towards her. I think that if she had been in a really large flock, worked with dogs and under much stress, she would long since have died of a heart attack!

Like Jesus lamenting over Jerusalem, I longed for her to trust and come to me... *"How often I would have gathered your children together, even as a hen gathers her chicks under her wings, but you would not"*. Matthew 23.37. I tried so hard to get her tame over the six years I kept her, and I was very disappointed because I loved her and yearned for her trust.

Naturally, she was very difficult to handle whenever we had to shear or dip the flock, tending to jump out of any pen. Her great fear was also transmitted to the rest of the sheep, so that she could panic all of them, even the tamest ewes.

Why did I keep her? Well, she had one redeeming feature; she was a marvellous mother and produced fine, strong lambs (always twins). She would have lots of milk so they grew well and she was very protective and attentive to them. But one year her innate distrust of me blotted out even these pluses in her favour. At lambing time she ran into trouble and it became obvious that she was in difficulties. Despite all our efforts at rounding everyone up, we were unable to catch her in time and as a result her lambs died. Both she and I were very upset - if only she had let me help her, then her "joy would have been full".

She preferred to follow the crowd and was always well behind the bunch. She could see no safety in me, her shepherd, and though she knew me and my voice, she did not want to follow me. So, when it came to the time when my husband became very ill and I had to reduce ewe numbers by half, you can imagine which list she was on. Although I often think of her, I am relieved that she is no longer here to disturb the peace and trust my smaller flock now enjoy.

In total contrast to Crazy Annie is Crappie. She like Annie, arrived as a timid ewe lamb of six months, when we bought in two dozen young ewes to expand our flock. For a few months, she hovered in the background, when I was fussing over my older ewes; she watched me but did not quite dare to come to me. However, once she had lambed, this seemed to make her bolder and she discovered the joy of being tickled under her arms and will now poke me with a hoof for this attention. She will leave everything, even her lambs, which she adores, and even her lovely grazing to come to me for a fuss. If I do not go to her on the field, I can feel her eyes burning on me as she stands, longing for me to call her over (she knows her name). She trusts me with her lambs and will readily let me help her if she is in difficulties at lambing. She is also one of the first to follow me when I call the flock and lead them to a new pasture.

She is truly a faithful servant, loving, trusting, obedient and a constant humbling reminder of what My Lord wants from me. She lives out Psalm 73.28 "*but as for me, it is good to be near God, I have put my trust in Him*", and I will never part with her.

THAT WAS THE WEEK, THAT WAS

It was only mid-May, but temperatures were already soaring in what was to be a blistering summer of total drought. So I was very glad that my shepherd friend, who is a skilled shearer, was free to see to my sheep. As he worked through the flock, we checked those few who had not lambed. The first one was a fat little ewe lamb, now a year old and a favourite of mine. She had been one of a set of orphaned triplets which I had had to bottle rear. Bess, as I had named her, had been served in the autumn by Sidney, but had no sign of an udder, so she was declared "definitely **not** in lamb", and sent off with the rest who had been sheared. Then we came to Tripper 5 Shear, who had given me a fine set of triplets every year until this one and now seemed barren. Her green bottom declared that she had taken the ram, but although she was very large, her udder was floppy and she was weeks past her due date. "Nooooo - not in lamb", was the verdict and off she went too. Lastly we came to Tiny Two, a retired old codger who had not been with a husband at all. **But,** two of the other oldies had lambed unexpectedly already - a ram-lamb must have jumped into their field one joyful night. So I had a feeling about Tiny Two, who seemed rather fat for such an old sheep. Again there was no real sign of her udder filling up, so I packed her off back to the geriatric ward in the small field by the house.

Thus lulled into a false sense of security, I had thoughts of putting my feet up for a while the next day, but by lunch time my confidence in our decisions was waning. My sheep have always been good at making a fool of me, so I felt that Tiny Two at least might have a surprise in store for me. The main flock were rather startled to see me in the middle of the day and didn't rally round as usual so I had to search for Bess and Tripper. The latter I found eating her head off, but Bess seemed to be agitated and trying to tell me something. On reaching her side, I nearly trod on a tiny lamb lying in the long grass. It was weakly and needed attention, so scooping it up, I called to Bess to follow. As we set off, a sudden movement to my right made me turn to see another small lamb scrabbling to its feet. Bess had had **twins**, a few hours ago -

as both were dry - such a double event is not common in ewe lambs who are not much more than babies themselves. Picking up infant number two as well we all went to the Sheep House, where I could make sure that the lambs were fed until Bess' udder really filled up.

Two days after Bess's happy event, as I went to the cattle to check their water tanks, I was amazed to find a heifer was calving. According to my calculations, she had another month to go but the fine calf she produced soon after was certainly not premature. So when I phoned a friend who was to buy her and baby as soon as she calved, I had to admit I had got my dates a bit wrong! As we were loading this family up the next evening, I became aware of urgent bleating. Someone in the main flock needed me, and once Mother and baby were in the trailer I went to the sheep. As I neared them, I realised it was Tripper's voice I could hear. This made me break into a run, because she had to be lambing after all. And sure enough when I reached her I found a large head hanging out and completely stuck. It was swelling very fast and urgent action was needed. There was no time to go the quarter of a mile back to the house for disinfectant and lubricant, so rolling up my sleeves, I set to at once. Tripper did not want to stand still, but somehow I reached both the lamb's legs and brought them out so that Tripper and I could deliver the baby. It was **very** large and fat and within ten minutes was up and sucking.

Of course you have guessed the rest. Tiny Two produced a fine Ram lamb by the weekend and despite her rheumatics, which means she can't stand for long, he has learned to dash in under her for a quick feed, or lie down with her and suck the teat which is uppermost. All the families have done well and each time I see them I laugh about the week I got everything wrong. I've suffered a bit of a blow to my confidence in my own judgment, because those three ewes and Thisby, the heifer, made me look a complete chump.

They must have known that I need to take the advice of Proverbs Chapter 3 to heart. "*Trust in the Lord..... and lean not on your own understanding*". I am sure God must have smiled about what happened that week, and He certainly reminded me of Paul's words to the Corinthians where he states "*Hasn't God made foolish the wisdom of the world?*" He who made the stars and "threw them into space" must laugh over the many scientific theories we are given as facts, only to find they have been disproved later on. It is so easy to be "wise in our own eyes" and think we have everything mapped out, even our futures. Whenever I am tempted to think like that, I know my sheep and cows will soon sort me out and put me in my place!